6-16

Understanding
PALESTINE
Today

Marcia Amidon Lusted

PALESTINE

Mitchell Lane
PUBLISHERS
P.O. Box 196
Hockessin, Delaware 19707

A Kid's Guide to THE MIDDLE EAST

Understanding Afghanistan Today
Understanding Iran Today
Understanding Iraq Today
Understanding Israel Today
Understanding Jordan Today
Understanding Lebanon Today
Understanding Palestine Today
Understanding Saudi Arabia Today
Understanding Syria Today
Understanding Turkey Today

PALESTINE

ISRAEL

TURKEY

SYRIA

LEBANON—

IRAQ

AFGHANISTAN

PALESTINE

IRAN

ISRAEL

JORDAN

SAUDI
ARABIA

Mitchell Lane
PUBLISHERS

Printing   1   2   3   4   5   6   7   8   9

Library of Congress Cataloging-in-Publication Data
Lüsted, Marcia Amidon.
 Understanding Palestine today / by Marcia Amidon Lusted.
    pages cm. — (A kid's guide to the Middle East)
 Includes bibliographical references and index.
 ISBN 978-1-61228-655-6 (library bound)
 1. Palestine—Juvenile literature. I. Title.
 DS118.L87 2015
 956.95'3—dc23
                                                                  2014008838
eBook ISBN: 9781612286785

DEDICATION: With thanks to J. Tedrowe Bonner for his knowledge and insights about Palestine, and to Murad Al-Kufash, who is working hard to create a sustainable agricultural future for his homeland.

PUBLISHER'S NOTE: The fictionalized narrative used in portions of this book is an aid to comprehension. This narrative is based on the author's extensive research as to what actually occurs in a child's life in Palestine. It is subject to interpretation and might not be indicative of every child's life in Palestine. It is representative of some children and is based on research the author believes to be accurate. Documentation of such research is contained on pp. 60–61.

The Internet sites referenced herein were active as of the publication date. Due to the fleeting nature of some web sites, we cannot guarantee they will all be active when you are reading this book.

To reflect current usage, we have chosen to use the secular era designations BCE ("before the common era") and CE ("of the common era") instead of the traditional designations BC ("before Christ") and AD (*anno Domini,* "in the year of the Lord").

PBP

CONTENTS

BOLD words in text can be found in the glossary

Introduction

Technically, Palestine is not a country. Many people call it the Palestinian Territories, while others refer to it as the Occupied Territories under the military control of Israel. But one thing is certain. This small area—the West Bank and the Gaza Strip, which together cover less than 2,400 square miles (6,200 square kilometers)—is one of the most fiercely fought-over parcels of land in world history. Palestine includes holy sites of three different religions—Christianity, Islam, and Judaism—and their believers have often gone to war.

The **conflict** between Palestinians and Israelis has raged since 1948, when Israel became an independent country. It continues to the present day, making Palestine one of the most

Hebron is one of the largest cities in Palestine.

violent places in the Middle East. The other countries in the region have become involved in political turmoil, diplomacy, negotiation, and military action.

And yet it is also the homeland of millions of Palestinians around the world, who even though they cannot live there, are determined that one day Palestine will be an actual country in its own right. Despite the conflict that frequently brings violence and property destruction, Palestine is also a place where families create strong ties, kids go to school and play, and people practice their religions—just like almost everywhere else in the world.

This Palestinian boy and his sister ride to school on a donkey.

CHAPTER 1
A Day in the Life

Bahaa is nine years old. He lives in Beit Lahia, a city of about 60,000 people located in the Gaza Strip. Although Bahaa lives in a part of the world very different from the United States, he does many of the same things during a normal day as American kids. Because his home is in an area where violence sometimes occurs, there are things that are different about his life.

Bahaa has two brothers and two sisters. He and his family live in what is a big house for Gaza. Their home is a second-floor apartment with five bedrooms, one bathroom, a kitchen, and a living room. His uncle's family lives on the ground level of the same house. The street by Bahaa's house is very busy, with lots of traffic from cars and donkey carts.

Like most Palestinian kids, Bahaa goes to school from Monday through Thursday. First he eats a breakfast of milk, tea, eggs, cheese, fava beans, yogurt, and **pita bread**. His school is a ten-minute walk from his house, although some kids ride bicycles to school. Many families don't have cars, so kids who can't walk or bike might have to take a taxi to school.

In most Palestinian towns, kids attend the same school from kindergarten through high school. In bigger towns and cities, there might be a separate school for grades 7 and up. School is free, and boys and girls go to separate schools. In most schools, boys are only taught by male teachers, and girls are only taught by female teachers. Bahaa has a more formal relationship with his teachers than other kids around the world do. He calls them by their formal title, which is Mr. or *Ustazz* (the name given to a Muslim scholar). Bahaa likes some classes better than others. "I do not like Arabic class; they ask for too much writing and it hurts my hand," he said. "I like the math teacher better. He is nicer to me, and I do not have to write a lot. I answer some of the questions in the class; it's easier to do the homework for math than Arabic."[1]

All kids in the same grade take the same classes. Students usually stay in the same room while their teachers rotate from classroom to classroom. Bahaa has homework every day, as

Some Palestinian children attend classes in temporary classrooms because their schools have been damaged or destroyed during fighting.

well as school projects. He also takes tests that are usually based on what he has memorized.

Bahaa goes home around 12:30, and eats lunch with his family. Lunch is usually the biggest meal of the day. Rice with beef, chicken or lamb and vegetables with sauce are a common meal. Bahaa also likes to snack on things like hummus (a dip made from chickpeas) and potato chips. His favorite drinks are cola and tea.

Then Bahaa does his homework, sometimes with help from his parents. Both his mother and father work, but they are usually home at the same time as their kids. Some kids, depending on where they live and what the political situation is like, might not have many opportunities to play outside. They stay inside instead and watch cartoons or play computer games or chess. Bahaa likes to ride his bike. He also plays soccer, basketball, or volleyball in the street with other neighborhood kids. Or they may play hide and seek, a game that his sisters can join. Most girls do not play soccer or anything else with boys who aren't their relatives.

He spends much of his time with his brothers and sisters. He watches over them and takes care of them. Family is very important to Bahaa. "I like my family a lot; they are always there," he explains. "Sometimes I am mad at my brother Zazzaa because he is younger and people like him more than they like me. But he always asks me for help, and I help him. If any kid beats him, I defend my brother and make sure he is okay. My sisters are nice to me; they take care of me a lot when

IN CASE YOU WERE WONDERING
Some of Bahaa's favorite foods are familiar to all children, such as potato chips, chocolates, and soft drinks.

Mom is not home. I live with a large family, and my cousins are good too, but sometimes we disagree."[2]

Fridays are a little different because kids do not have school. Their parents are also home. Because almost everyone in Gaza is a believer in the religion of Islam, Bahaa goes to his local **mosque** for noon prayers with his father and then comes home for lunch. After eating, they often visit relatives or other families. Bahaa is sometimes invited to play with his cousins, or he visits his grandparents. If he is given spending money, he buys snacks and candy. The day ends with a light meal before bedtime.

Bahaa is old enough to know that he lives in a place that can be violent and dangerous. While his parents have not specifically told him about the war and **occupation** that are part of living in Palestine, he sees some of it for himself. He knows that his father stays awake long after his kids are asleep to make sure everything is fine. He also knows that his mother will sleep in the same room with them when his father is away.[3] "Every now and then there's violence in our area and we hear guns," Bahaa says. "I got scared when I was younger, but now that I am older, they do not scare me a lot. I try to make sure my younger sister is okay. I do not like to see guns, but the police have big ones."[4]

Unfortunately, there is no foreseeable end to this situation. The conflict between Palestinians and Israelis has endured for decades. Even getting the two sides to sit down and talk together has often proved to be virtually impossible.

IN CASE YOU WERE WONDERING

In the Islamic religion, boys and girls, and men and women who are not related to each other do not spend time alone together or touch.

THE REALITY OF BEING
A KID IN PALESTINE

The reality for children in Palestine is that they live in a very dangerous place. According to both the Palestine Ministry of Information and the United Nations, a total of 1,518 Palestinian children have been killed by Israeli forces in military actions and random violence since 2000. That's the equivalent of one child being killed every three days. During this same period, more than 6,000 children have been injured.[5]

Some of these children were killed while they were collecting stones in the border area between Gaza and Israel.[6] They were trying to help their families rebuild destroyed homes.

Teens who fight back against Israeli forces are often shot. As one visitor to Palestine noted, "If you throw a rock at a car in the United States, you might go to jail. If you throw a rock at a car in Palestine, you might get shot."[7] Some children under the age of 18 are also kept in Israeli prisons.

Even if they aren't caught up in violence, the United Nations reports that Palestinian children are more likely to suffer from fear and distress because of where they live. Their lives have changed dramatically in recent years, with fears of darkness, sleeping alone, strangers, loud noises, and even sudden movements.[8]

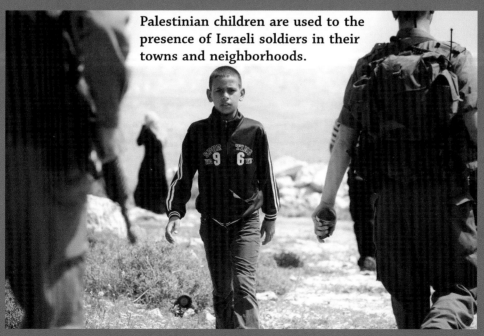

Palestinian children are used to the presence of Israeli soldiers in their towns and neighborhoods.

Palestinian workers gather the fruit from the tops of date palms, which grow in the Gaza Strip.

CHAPTER 2
Looking Around

Palestinian territory consists of two parts. One part is the Gaza Strip. It is a narrow sliver of land, about 25 miles (40 kilometers) long and between four and seven-and-a-half miles wide (6–12 km). Its total area is 140 square miles (360 square km), about twice the size of Washington, DC. Its borders are the Mediterranean Sea to the west, Israel on the north and the east, and Egypt to the south.

The land is almost entirely a flat or slightly rolling plain, with frequent areas of sand and sand dunes. Its highest point is only 345 feet (105 meters). Its location and terrain have been key elements in understanding its history. "With the Negev Desert to the south, the Sinai Desert to the southwest, the Mediterranean Sea to the west and the coastal plain leading to Syria to the north, it was the strategic point to launch offensives against Egypt, and Gaza's history has always been closely intertwined with that of Egypt," historians Rania Filfil and Barbara Louton note. "Gaza's native population has been subjected to many rulers and many occupations, some more brutal than others."[1]

The area has dry summers that are warm or even hot, and mild winters. Gaza has several environmental threats, with some areas becoming desert as sand creeps into the area, and fresh water becoming salty as salt water from the Mediterranean seeps into underground water supplies. Years of farming have also worn out the soil here. Only a small part is suitable for growing crops.

By far the largest city is Gaza City, with a population of more than 830,000. It is one of the longest-inhabited cities in the world, dating back to an Egyptian fortress established about 3000 BCE.

The other part of Palestine is the West Bank. It gets its name because it lies west of the Jordan River, which forms its eastern border. It shares the rest of its border with Israel. The West Bank is 80 miles (130 km) long and its width ranges from 25 miles (40 km) to 40 miles (65 km). Its total land area of 2,262 square miles (5,860 square km) is slightly smaller than Delaware.

The West Bank has four different regions. The Jordan River Valley, at the eastern edge, has been farmed for thousands of years. West of this valley is the eastern slopes area, which has rugged terrain with hills running north to south. With little rainfall, it is not a good area for growing crops, but many farmers use it for grazing sheep and goats. The central highlands form the spine of the West Bank where most of the population lives today. It receives enough rainfall for many different types of crops to grow well. Finally, there is the semi-coastal region which is near the shores of the Mediterranean Sea. It is flat and gets relatively little rainfall, so farmers need irrigation to grow crops. Environmental issues in the West Bank include lack of fresh water and **sewage** treatment facilities.[2]

Hebron is the largest city in the West Bank, with a population of about 160,000. The West Bank also has over 300 communities of Israelis who have settled there, creating conflict over land ownership and use.

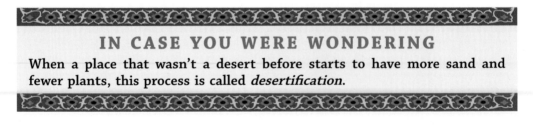

IN CASE YOU WERE WONDERING
When a place that wasn't a desert before starts to have more sand and fewer plants, this process is called *desertification*.

In total, Palestine includes 2,402 square miles of land (6,220 square km) and has a population of about four and a half million people. About 2,700,000 of them live in the West Bank, while slightly over 1,700,000 live in the Gaza Strip.[3] In addition, at least 340,000 Israeli settlers live in the West Bank.

Even though Palestine is a small area with many people, some wild animals live there. In fact, there are 116 different species, including wild boar, foxes, ibex, and mountain gazelles. There are also leopards, hyenas, jackals, and wolves, but these are not seen very often. The number of animals in each species is shrinking, and some animals that are used to migrating no longer can because of walls and border gates. There are also 470 species of birds in Palestine, and millions of birds follow a **migration** path across the area every year.

The Nubian Ibex is one of the wild animals found in the West Bank.

Palestine has several famous landmarks, especially those related to the different religions with sacred sites there. For example, Bethlehem is the site of the Christian Church of the Nativity, built on the site where Jesus is said to have been born. Because Palestine has been settled for thousands of years, there are remains of many ancient cities and seaports. The Erq al-Ahmar cave near Bethlehem was inhabited by prehistoric people as long as 50,000 years ago. Other natural landmarks include two oak trees—the al-Badawi near Jerusalem and the Oak of Mamre near Hebron in the West Bank—which may be more than 5,000 years old!

The Church of the Nativity in Bethlehem is sacred to Christians because it is believed to be on the site where Jesus was born.

THE DEAD SEA

Part of the West Bank territory includes the Dead Sea. Located in a valley surrounded by the West Bank, Jordan, and Israel, the Dead Sea is 31 miles long (50 km) and nine miles wide (15 km). Because it is 1,401 feet (427 meters) below sea level, it is the lowest point on dry land on earth. It is incredibly salty, nine times saltier than the ocean.

Because it is so salty, plants and marine creatures can't survive in the Dead Sea, which is how it got its name. However, the salty water makes it extremely easy for swimmers to float in the Dead Sea's waters with almost no effort![4]

Starting in the time of King Herod the Great in the first century BCE, the Dead Sea became noted for its healing properties. Economists believe that building health-oriented resorts on the Palestinian shoreline could generate hundreds of millions of dollars in revenue, but thus far Palestinians haven't been able to obtain the necessary permits.

Environmentalists are concerned that the water levels in the Dead Sea have been steadily dropping as Israel and Jordan divert larger amounts of water from the Jordan River—which flows into the Dead Sea—for irrigation. The government of Jordan recently announced plans to pump water from the Red Sea into the country. Part of it would be diverted to the Dead Sea.

Because there is so much salt in the Dead Sea, people are able to float easily.

The city of Jerusalem is built on the remains of Roman, Christian, Jewish, and Muslim settlements. Elements of each can still be seen in the city today.

CHAPTER 3
A Land at the Crossroads

From ancient times, Palestine has been a battleground because of its central location among African, Asian, and European cultures. Many great empires have fought to control it, including Egypt, Rome, the Byzantines, and the Ottomans. It is also sacred to three different religions—Christians, Jews, and Muslims—who refer to it as the Holy Land.

Around 1000 BCE, the Jews—or Hebrews, as they were more commonly known at that time—established the kingdom of Israel in modern-day Palestine and built a temple in its capital city of Jerusalem. The kingdom later split into two states called Israel and Judah, which were conquered by several different empires. In 587 Babylonia destroyed the temple in Jerusalem and took most of the Jews into captivity. Though they returned several decades later and rebuilt the temple, the area was conquered again by the Greeks, then the Romans in the first century BCE. After several revolts, Roman soldiers destroyed the rebuilt temple and drove nearly all of the Jews out in what became known as the Diaspora. The Romans renamed the region as Syria Palestina to show that the Jews no longer had any connection to the land.

Shortly after the Prophet Muhammad founded the religion of Islam in the early 600s, Arab Muslim armies took over Palestine and allowed Jews to return after more than five centuries of banishment. Despite brief periods of Christian control, Arabs ruled the region until it became part of the Ottoman Empire—which was also based on Islam—in the sixteenth century.

Members of the First Crusade rejoice at their first sight of Jerusalem in 1099. They captured it soon afterward, believing that the Holy Land should belong to Christians.

IN CASE YOU WERE WONDERING

In 1096, European Christian knights began the First Crusade, which captured Jerusalem and the rest of the Holy Land. But an Arab military leader named Saladin defeated the Christians in 1187 and restored Muslim control. Several additional Crusades failed to retake the Holy Land.

Starting in the late 1800s, Jews fleeing increasing persecution in Europe began coming to Palestine. In 1897, the Jewish movement known as Zionism declared that its ultimate aim was to establish a Jewish homeland in the Holy Land. Many of the newcomers purchased land from the Ottoman owners. While Jews and Arabs lived in relative peace, some Arabs were becoming increasingly uneasy. Ruhi Khalidi, a member of a prominent family in Jerusalem, warned that "The aim of the Zionists is the creation of an Israeli kingdom whose capital will be Jerusalem."[1]

When World War I started in 1914, Great Britain, France, Russia, and eventually the United States fought against Germany, Austria-Hungary, and the Ottoman Empire, which still controlled Palestine. British troops moved into Palestine during the war, but they needed allies to firm up their control. In 1917, the British issued the Balfour Declaration, which encouraged the formation of a Jewish state in Palestine:

> His Majesty's Government view with favor the establishment in Palestine of a national home for the Jewish people, and will use their best endeavors to facilitate the achievement of this object, it being clearly understood that nothing shall be done which may prejudice the civil and religious rights of existing non-Jewish communities in Palestine, or the rights and political status enjoyed by Jews in any other country.[2]

At the same time, the British were promising the Arabs that they too could have control over the region, as well as other parts of the Ottoman Empire. After the war, the League of Nations—an early version of the United Nations—**mandated** that Britain should govern Palestine. At the same time, Arab Palestinians were becoming more interested in their culture, heritage, and traditions. This Palestinian nationalism fed their desire for political independence and a country of their own.

However, the Jews were better prepared for the creation of a new nation than the Palestinians. They had already set up a kind of Zionist government agency to oversee affairs there. Zionists were also encouraging even more Jews to immigrate to the area and purchase land. The agency also organized a group of labor unions for construction projects, and took over Jewish schools to make sure that Palestinian Jews would learn to speak Hebrew as a show of unity.

The differing goals quickly led to conflict and a series of riots between Arabs and Jews. The first riot took place in Jerusalem in 1920, with nine people killed. More riots followed in succeeding years, with even more people killed each time.

As the Nazi Party became more powerful in Germany in the early 1930s, Jews were being persecuted and imprisoned. Many fled. By 1936, a quarter million Jews had **immigrated** to Palestine. That same year, Palestinian Arabs revolted against both the British and those Jews who wanted their own state. Arab leaders called for a general strike and a **boycott** of Jewish products. There were terrorist attacks and more riots. The British sent the Peel Commission to Palestine to investigate the situation the following year. The Commission recommended dividing Palestine into two states, a small one for Jews and a much larger one for Arabs. The Arabs refused to consider the idea and the rioting continued. The riots finally ended shortly before the start of World War II in September, 1939. More than 5,000 Arabs died as a result of the three years of unrest.

There were several consequences. On the one hand, with storm clouds developing over Europe, the British wanted to encourage the Arabs to remain on their side in the upcoming conflict. So they reversed the Balfour Declaration in what is called the White Paper of 1939. It said, "His Majesty's Government therefore now declare unequivocally that it is not part of their policy that Palestine should become a Jewish State."[3] It went on to promise an Arab Palestinian state after the war, and halted further Jewish immigration into Palestine. And as historian Esmail Nashif observes, the revolt is "credited with signifying the birth of the Arab Palestinian identity."[4]

On the other hand, the British killed, captured, or exiled many of the Palestinian leaders. They also encouraged Jewish militia forces to help them suppress the revolt. Those forces received invaluable training and actual battlefield experience which would be of immense value in the following years.

After the end of World War II, the British continued to try to balance the Jewish and Arab claims to Palestine. They were no more successful than they had been before the war. Finally they turned the problem over to the newly formed United Nations. Many member nations had been shocked by the Holocaust, the systematic murder of millions of Jews by Germany. That made them receptive to the idea of a Jewish homeland. Late in 1947, the UN voted to divide Palestine into separate Jewish and Arab states. While the territory allotted to the Jews was larger than the Arab portion, much of it consisted of the Negev Desert where few people lived. The city of Jerusalem was given a separate status as an international zone because it was so important to both groups. The Jews accepted the vote. The Arab Palestinians didn't. Jewish leader David Ben-Gurion understood their feelings. "Sure, God promised [Palestine] to us, but what does that matter to them [the Arabs]?" he explained. "There has been anti-Semitism, the Nazis, Hitler, Auschwitz [a prison camp where many Jews were killed in World War II], but was that their fault? They only see one thing: We have come here and stolen their country."[5]

Almost immediately the two sides began fighting each other. "On paper and on the ground, the Palestinians had the edge: there were twice as many of them, they occupied the higher altitudes and they had friendly regimes next door," notes journalist David Margolick. "But isolated and outnumbered as

IN CASE YOU WERE WONDERING

The German Nazi Party believed that all Jews should be killed because they were responsible for Germany's problems, and because they belonged to an inferior race. Both beliefs were false.

David Ben-Gurion gives a speech on May 14, 1948, declaring the creation of the State of Israel. The photo behind him is Theodor Herzl, the founder of Zionism.

they were, the Jews were far better organized, motivated, financed, equipped and trained than their adversaries, who were so fragmented—by geography and tradition and clan— that the term 'Palestinian' was either unwarranted or at least premature."[6] Both sides had initial successes—the Arabs nearly succeeded in starving Jerusalem into submission by cutting off supplies from reaching the city for several months—but by mid-May of the following year the Jews had the upper hand. On May 14, 1948, the new Jewish state of Israel declared its independence.

JERUSALEM

Jerusalem was first settled in 3500 BCE. King David made it the capital of the new country of Israel about 2,500 years later, and his son Solomon built a temple on Temple Mount. That temple was eventually destroyed, rebuilt, and destroyed again. All that remains today of those temples is the Western Wall, one of the holiest sites of the Jewish religion.

Jerusalem became holy to Christians because much of Jesus's ministry took place in the city and the surrounding region. Christians especially venerate the Church of the Holy Sepulchre, which they believe marks the location of his crucifixion and burial place.

When Muhammad founded the religion of Islam, its adherents originally prayed in the direction of Jerusalem. Muslims also believe that one of the most important events in Muhammad's life, the Night Journey, took place in Jerusalem in the year 621. Riding a horse-like creature named Buraq, Muhammad ascended to heaven and met God. The Al-Aqsa Mosque, the starting point of the journey, and an adjoining shrine called the Dome of the Rock were built on Temple Mount, becoming the third-holiest site in Islam.

Jerusalem is therefore important to all three of these religions. This importance was the major reason why Jerusalem itself was not included in either territory when Israel and Palestine were separated in 1948.

Much of modern-day Jerusalem lies on top of ruins of an earlier version of the city. Construction of buildings today is often halted because of the discovery of **archaeological** remains.

A view of Temple Mount in the old city of Jerusalem with the Western Wall and golden Dome of the Rock

This Palestinian boy, wearing a traditional keffiyah headdress, holds a sign shaped like a key with the words "We will return for sure."

CHAPTER 4
Conflict and Occupation

As soon as Israel declared its independence, five neighboring Arab countries—Egypt, Iraq, Lebanon, Syria, and Jordan—launched attacks on the new nation. Initially the two sides were roughly equivalent in manpower, though the Arab armies enjoyed a substantial advantage in artillery, armored vehicles, and aircraft. After giving up some territory at the start of the conflict, Israeli forces pushed back the invaders as they began acquiring their own heavy weapons. They were also much better organized than their opponents, who rarely coordinated their efforts. When the fighting ended 10 months later, Israel had not only secured the territory granted by the UN but also taken about 60 percent of the land originally allocated to the Palestinians. Arab countries took over the remainder. Jordan controlled the West Bank (as well as part of Jerusalem) and Egypt controlled the Gaza Strip.

This loss of their homeland was called *al-Nakba* ("the disaster") by the Arab Palestinians. During and after the war, about three-quarters of a million Palestinians fled to the West Bank, the Gaza Strip, and nearby Arab countries. Many thought they would return once the fighting was over, but Israel passed laws denying them the right to come back and often seized their property. Only about 150,000 Palestinians remained in Israel.

This began an ongoing struggle between the Israelis and the Palestinians over land. Many of the Palestinians who had to flee to other countries continued to push for a Palestinian homeland they could return to. Palestinians did find a voice when the Palestine Liberation Organization (PLO) was established in 1964. Egypt **sponsored** the PLO as a way to coordinate the activities of different groups working to create an independent Palestinian country.

In 1967, Israel fought the Six-Day War against Egypt, Syria, and Jordan. Israel defeated the Arabs and captured the West Bank and the Gaza Strip. Israel also **annexed** (added to its territory) East Jerusalem, a holy place for Muslims, Christians, and Jews.

The Arab loss in the Six-Day War made the PLO stronger. Palestinians decided that the only way to fight for their cause was to do it themselves. In 1969, Yasser Arafat began leading the PLO. He had founded another group, the al-Fatah (victory party), in 1959. Arafat became the closest thing to a national leader that the Palestinians had.

Other countries and the United Nations tried to create peace between Israel and the Palestinians, but these peace talks broke down. Israelis were also starting to build their own settlements in the Palestinian Territories, which were not officially part of Israel but were controlled by them. The settlers took land away from Palestinians and forced them to live somewhere else. Israel also controlled the Palestinians living in the West Bank and Gaza Strip. They regulated the materials and supplies that went into or came out of the two areas. They restricted what kinds of businesses Palestinians could run. Many Palestinians were forced to work for Israelis, often at low-wage jobs. They also had to pass through military **checkpoints**

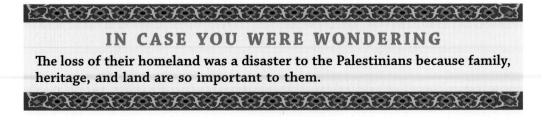

IN CASE YOU WERE WONDERING

The loss of their homeland was a disaster to the Palestinians because family, heritage, and land are so important to them.

every day to go to those jobs in Israeli areas. Tensions between the two sides steadily increased.

On December 8, 1987, an Israeli truck driver in the Gaza Strip made a wrong turn and barreled into incoming traffic. Four Palestinian workers were killed. Instantly there were rumors among Palestinians that the deaths were revenge for an Israeli businessman who had been stabbed to death in Gaza two days earlier. Some young Palestinians living in a refugee camp began throwing rocks at Israeli soldiers, who shot one of them. Riots and demonstrations quickly spread, launching what was soon called the Intifada. Young Palestinians threw rocks at Israeli troops, who fired back with rubber bullets and tear gas. Other Palestinians went on strike, boycotted Israeli goods, and even quit their jobs working for Israelis. It made life even harder for Palestinians, but it also united them as a community and made them stronger. It also showed the Israelis that the Palestinians were not ready to accept Israeli occupation and give up their dream of a land of their own. The violence continued to escalate, and eventually the Israelis used live ammunition.

The world was surprised in 1993 when the PLO and Israeli leaders announced that they had been holding secret peace talks in Oslo, Norway. They had agreed on the Israeli-Palestinian Peace Accord that would hopefully bring peace to the region by giving the Palestinians a limited amount of power to rule themselves in the Palestinian Territories. A governing group called the Palestinian National Authority (PNA) was created in 1994, with Arafat as its leader. Palestinians also elected an 88-member Palestinian Council.

Unfortunately these peace efforts broke down. Each side accused the other of being at fault. The Second Intifada began in 2000 with more protests and violence. When Arafat died in

Palestinian leader Yasser Arafat and Palestinian Prime Minister Mahmoud Abbas attend an executive committee meeting in Arafat's office in August 2003, in the West Bank city of Ramallah. Abbas became the Palestinian leader when Arafat died on November 11, 2004.

2004, he was replaced by Mahmoud Abbas. Tensions continued between Palestinians and Israelis, often resulting in protests and bloodshed. In 2005, Israel withdrew from the Gaza Strip, hoping to reduce the friction. However, many Palestinians still regard this area as being occupied by Israel.

In 2011, President Barack Obama called for peace between the two sides. He thought a peace treaty should include swapping land, based on the borders before the 1967 war. His words had very little effect. Israel, Jordan, and the Palestinian Authority did sign an agreement two years later to create a new source of fresh water in the region. But other political and economic problems continue.

TERRORISM IN PALESTINE AND ISRAEL

In the years leading up to the creation of the state of Israel in 1948, both sides employed terrorist tactics against their opponents. After the Six-Day War, some Palestinian groups realized they couldn't confront Israel militarily. They increasingly began targeting civilians, both in Israel and in the outside world, for terror attacks which included hijacking, bombing, and kidnapping.

One notorious attack came at the 1972 Olympic Games in Munich, Germany. A group called Black September murdered 11 Israeli athletes and coaches. Another one came in 1985 when Palestinians took over a cruise ship named the *Achille Lauro*. They shot a wheelchair-bound American named Leon Klinghoffer and threw his body overboard.

Some terrorist organizations say that their actions are justified by Islam. **Jihads**, which are acts of violence used to retaliate or avenge acts that have supposedly hurt Muslims, are carried out against countries and leaders who are seen as being anti-Islamic.

The most important Islamic terror group in Palestine is Hamas, which emerged during the First Intifada. Suicide bombings directed against Israelis were one of their most effective tactics. More recently, Hamas assumed control of the Gaza Strip and there have been few terror attacks.

Such Islamic extremist groups do not represent all Muslims. They may be dangerous, but

Israeli armored vehicles approach the Palestine border to fight against Hamas militants on January 7, 2009.

they are a minority. According to Noha Aboulmagd-Forster, a professor of Arabic at the University of Chicago, "you have the huge billion-person-strong Muslim community, people who certainly don't believe that there is some duty to go and fight Christians or Jews."[1]

The village of Al-Issawiya is an Arab neighborhood in Jerusalem. It has a population of 15,000.

CHAPTER 5
Living in Palestine

For Palestinians, home is very important. It is a connection to their traditions and their history, and a place where strong family bonds are created. Often parents will buy neighboring houses so their sons will have homes for their future families.

Palestinians live in several different kinds of housing. Some live in refugee camps that have become permanent settlements with cinder-block huts and **corrugated** iron roofs. Families cook on metal grates placed over charcoal fires. Beds are thin mats on the floor. Metal drums with water drawn from a community well are used for bathing and washing clothing.

Some Palestinians live on small farms. Their homes may have modern conveniences or they may be older and more traditional, without electricity or running water. Many farms have walls to keep stray animals out of crops, especially wild pigs that have been released into the countryside. In traditional villages, most houses are only one story and made from traditional white stone. They may have just a kitchen, living room, bathroom, and several small bedrooms.

These houses are surrounded by walls with a gate, and have gardens. Family members live close to each other, often with the grandparents' house in the center, where most of the family events take place. People who have more money may live in two-story homes, with the living area on the second floor and the bottom floor for storage and utilities. Other Palestinians live in modern towns and have comfortable homes. Most homes have indoor plumbing and electricity and modern appliances. However, especially in the Gaza Strip, garbage and sewage systems are usually not good.

Even though Palestinians value owning their own home, land in cities is more and more expensive. Palestinians in cities often live in apartment buildings, at least while they save money to buy a home. The average apartment is not large, with just a living room, kitchen, bathroom, balcony, and several bedrooms. There is usually one bedroom for the parents and one each for male and female children.

Unfortunately, many Palestinian homes have been destroyed by Israeli forces. Homes may be bulldozed, blown up, or burned down. Sometimes families are only given a few moments to get out of their houses before they are destroyed. Often Palestinian families have no choice except to live in tents or move to refugee camps. In 2013, that number reached an all-time high as 663 homes and buildings were torn down. Many of these were destroyed to make way for more Israeli settlements. Sometimes Israeli officials claimed that the homes were built without proper permits.

Palestinians aren't just those who physically live in Palestine. There are actually four groups of Palestinians. One is the people who stayed in Israel after the 1948 division of the area—even though they are not Jewish—and their **descendants**. Second are the Palestinians who actually live in the Gaza Strip and the West Bank, owning their own land and homes. Third are Palestinians who had to flee from the wars that took place in 1948 and 1967, and may live in refugee camps in the Palestinian

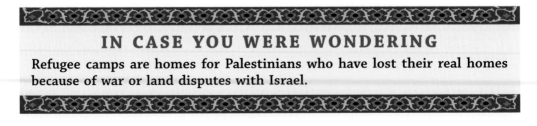

IN CASE YOU WERE WONDERING

Refugee camps are homes for Palestinians who have lost their real homes because of war or land disputes with Israel.

Territories or in neighboring countries such as Jordan, Lebanon, or Syria. Fourth are Palestinians who fled even further to other countries, such as the United States. But even though they may not all be physically living in Palestine, they are all Palestinians.

Before 1948, most Palestinians lived in villages and farmed their land. Each *hara* (a village, neighborhood, or quarter) was led by an elected *mukhtar*, who was responsible for administrative details, recording births and deaths, and settling disputes. He ruled over the *hamoula*, a group with representatives from each family in the village or neighborhood. This same kind of organization has been used in Palestinian refugee camps and city neighborhoods, especially now that many Palestinians have moved into cities and away from farms and villages. They have also started to adapt to Western culture and values. Palestinians who have returned home from Western countries have brought some of these values with them. Because they have political or social connections, these "returnees" often get the best-paying jobs. They often have nice homes, several cars, and maids. They can also move more easily between Palestine and other places. This makes the Palestinians who have always lived in the Gaza Strip and West Bank resentful.

At one time Palestinians were also divided by what class they belonged to. Some belonged to the upper class, some to the middle class (merchants and tradesmen), and some to the labor (working) class. Upper class members had more political influence and better economic resources. However, the middle and labor classes are gaining more power now. There are also gaps between Palestinians who live in the country, those who live in cities, and those who live in refugee camps.

Palestine's economy is still mostly based on agriculture. Farms, many of them located around small villages in the West Bank, produce olives, grains, fruits, and vegetables. On the Gaza Strip, crops are mostly citrus fruits and vegetables. Fishing and raising animals are also important parts of the economy. Most of the fruits, vegetables, and things like cooking oil are sold to Israel. There are some small industries which make items that

A Palestinian shepherd tends to his flock of sheep near the West Bank village of Sebastia.

A Palestinian woman collects fallen olives from the ground as her family harvest their olives near their village of Hawarra in the West Bank. Olives are an important part of Palestinian life. They are eaten as is, pressed into olive oil to last all season and to sell, and the leftover husks after pressing are used for fuel.

are mostly sold to Israel. These are mostly cloth, cement, toys, furniture, clothing, shoes, and processed foods.

Many Palestinians depend on Israel or neighboring Arab states for jobs. Many of the Palestinians who live in the Gaza Strip commute to jobs in Israel. Some work in service jobs, such as hotels or restaurants, while many also work in construction. But after the intifadas, jobs in Israel became much harder to get for Palestinians. When Palestinian workers went on strike in support of the intifadas, many were fired and replaced with workers from other countries. Palestinians who worked in neighboring countries that produced oil lost their jobs because they supported Iraq during the Persian Gulf War in 1991.

Overall, the economies of both the West Bank and Gaza are poor and continue to struggle. Many people are either unemployed or underemployed, which means they aren't working as much as they'd like or in jobs that are not a good fit for their abilities. When workers can't reach their jobs in Israel because of border closings, they can't work and the economy suffers. The standard of living there is decreasing, and many of the most skilled and educated workers are being forced to leave Palestine altogether.[1]

Currently, the two parts of Palestine are ruled by two different groups. The Gaza Strip is governed by an Islamic militant group called Hamas. A prime minister heads Hamas and appoints ministers to help him govern the social, political, and military branches of the government. The West Bank is governed by the Palestinian National Authority, headed by a president who serves for a four-year term. There is also a prime minister, appointed by the president, and a Palestinian Legislative Council (PLC) with 132 members. This group has not been able to function since 2007 because of disagreements between the Palestinian Authority, the PA's leading political party Fatah, and the ruling Gaza group Hamas. It has also become too difficult for Parliament members to move between Gaza and the West Bank. Israel still controls security and borders in the West Bank. However, in 2013, Hamas and the Palestinian Authority met to discuss forming a unified government to rule all parts of Palestine.[2]

The United Nations recognizes both the West Bank and the Gaza Strip as Palestine, and in 2012 Palestine was invited to be a permanent observer of United Nations proceedings. It is the first step to recognizing Palestine as a country.

THE ISRAELI WALL

In 2002, during the Second Intifada, Israel began to build a security barrier along the borders of the West Bank. According to the International Court of Justice, "The construction of the wall being built by Israel, the occupying Power, in the Occupied Palestinian Territory, including in and around East Jerusalem, and its associated régime, are contrary to international law."[3] The Israeli government insisted that it was necessary to protect people from Palestinian suicide bombers.

Most of the barrier consists of fencing surrounded by deep trenches to stop vehicles. About 10 percent is a concrete wall 26 feet (8 meters) high.

However, instead of strictly following the border, the barrier curves in and out of the West Bank. Sometimes it goes miles inside of it. Eighty-five percent of the wall is on Palestinian property, and many Palestinians have lost part of their land, which is now on the other side of the wall. Farmers have been separated from part of their farms. Kids can no longer walk to their schools, and some families can no longer visit their relatives. Checkpoints allow Palestinians to pass through, but they are far apart and only open at certain times.

Palestinians have started using the wall for messages and for artwork. Some share information and invite others to protests. Some paintings are meant to raise awareness of the Palestinian cause. Others paint Palestinian symbols like flags and olive trees. Some artists have painted beautiful landscape murals.

Palestinians often paint murals on the Israeli Wall to express their frustration and to protest against Israeli occupation. This section of wall is located near the Aida refugee camp.

These Palestinian women are wearing traditional clothing of long robes and headscarves.

CHAPTER 6
At Home

One of the first things to notice about daily life in Palestine is language. Palestinian Arabs speak Arabic (while their neighbors, the Israelis, speak Hebrew) and have their own **dialect** known as Palestinian. However, most news broadcasts, newspapers, and government speeches use regular Arabic. Many Palestinians also speak English or French as well.

Palestinians in urban areas generally wear Western-style clothing, and young people often wear jeans and T-shirts. Older people might wear more traditional clothing. For men, long, loose white robes and a *keffiyah*, a scarf with a black-and-white checked pattern unique to Palestinians, are common. Women might wear traditional embroidered dresses. Most women, old and young, cover their hair with a scarf. After the First Intifada, some urban women went back to wearing more traditional clothing like long loose-fitting dresses and even veils to show support for those who died in the conflict.

Palestinians are known not only for their strong family ties and their values of courage, freedom, generosity, and hospitality, but also for their sociability. When they pass each other in the street, they generally smile and nod. They often exchange greetings like *Al-salam alaykum* ("Peace be upon you") or *Ma al-salameh*, *deer balak* ("Goodbye, take care"). Women or close friends might also greet each other with a handshake, hug, and kiss on the cheek, but for religious reasons men and women who aren't related to each other only exchange spoken greetings when they meet.

Palestinians like to visit each other for special occasions or just to socialize. Relatives often stop by each other's houses unannounced. Guests usually bring gifts like flowers or chocolates. In homes where conservative rules are followed, men and women sit in different rooms while they visit. Men might also visit coffee shops called *qahweh*, where they can talk about current events, religion, and their society while they drink coffee or tea and play cards. Women who live in rural areas might gather for morning coffee before they prepare lunch.

Because of border checkpoints and other political issues that make travel difficult, most Palestinians do not take vacations. Instead, they visit nearby places, such as ancestral villages or the homes of relatives. In the summer, they may go to the beach. Palestinians who live in the city might take trips into the countryside, go shopping, eat at restaurants, dance, or attend parties. They might also go to concerts or art galleries. Many people stay home and have barbecues, where they gather with family and friends for socializing, eating, and music.

The roles of men and women are more traditional than in Western countries. The father is the head of the household. The mother can work outside of the home, and she usually takes care of the house and the children. If she does have a job, it might be in a career such as teaching, where it is easier to balance work and family. Or she might have a skill or craft that can be done at home and then sold. Boys are expected to help their fathers, while girls help with household chores. Young

IN CASE YOU WERE WONDERING

Keffiyahs were originally used to keep the harsh desert sun off the face and neck. It is a square scarf, sometimes held in place with a circle of rope or cord.

A Palestinian family, including several generations, relaxes in their home.

people usually live with their families until they are married. While divorce is not socially accepted, a woman who gets divorced may return to her parents' home with her children. Ties between parents and children are very close, and boys are expected to protect their sisters and care for them and their mother if necessary.

When children finish school, they must pass a final exam to attend college. A college education is very important to Palestinians, even though it is expensive and does not guarantee a job. Unemployment is high in Palestine, up to 50 percent or more. Even college graduates may go months without a job or a regular salary. Boys might leave to find work. Girls also attend university, but they are more likely to return home afterwards. A young woman named Hanadi provides an example. She is 24 and is finished with school. She still lives at home, but she has much more freedom than her mother did. "In comparison to my mom's life, I think in my time it's easier for a girl to go out, study at college, and work," she explained. "My mom, after graduating from high school, couldn't go out for college/ university. At that time it was not common for girls to travel and leave their families' houses to go and study."[1]

Most Palestinians believe that the best thing is to be in Palestine. As Murad Al-Kufash, who has a farm in Marda Village, stated, "The best thing is my homeland, generations of family, the soil and trees irrigated by the blood of people who have lived there."[2] Palestinians are taught from birth to cherish their heritage and respect the elderly. In their culture, old people should not die angry or upset, so they live with their families until death, and their families do what they can to keep them happy.

What kinds of foods do Palestinians enjoy? While Palestinians who are strict Muslims cannot eat pork or drink alcohol, there are plenty of other choices. Vegetables, rice, beef, and lamb are a part of almost every meal. Chicken, fish, garbanzo beans, fava beans, oranges, grapes, dates, figs, and olives are also common. There are many traditional dishes. *Mansaf* is made of rice, lamb, yogurt, bread, and nuts. A dish of bread with fried onions and chicken on top (*musakhan*) and stuffed grape leaves (*waraq dawalee*) are also popular. Couscous, a kind of wheat pasta, is served with vegetables and meat in a dish called *maftool*, or there is *maqlubah* (vegetables, meat, and rice served with yogurt and salad). *Falafel*, a mixture of crushed garbanzo beans mixed with oil and spices, made into balls and fried, is often served as a filling for pita bread. Most Palestinians drink tea, coffee, fruit juice, and soft drinks.

For dessert, there are baklava, figs in syrup, rice pudding with rosewater, *harissah* (a coconut cake), *ghraybeh* (sugar cookies), and *fteer* (pastries stuffed with sweet cheese or cream). A particular favorite is *qatayef*, pancakes stuffed with cheese or walnuts, then baked and dipped in a sugar syrup.

A PERMACULTURE FARM

In 2006, Palestinian Murad Al-Kufash established the Marda Permaculture Farm in the village of Marda in the West Bank. Permaculture is a combination of the words "permanent" and "agriculture." It refers to a system of designing landscapes that produce food while conserving water, energy, and other resources.

Because Palestine suffers from food shortages and the resulting high prices, the Marda Farm's mission is to teach Palestinians how to produce more of their own food on small farms using organic methods. It also uses farming knowledge passed down through generations. "We believe that permaculture is a key ingredient in the future, not only for Palestine, but for the Middle East and the world," as Al-Kufash notes. "We're setting out to show how it's done."[3]

People from all over the world visit the farm to learn more about permaculture and growing food. They can learn techniques as diverse as making solar ovens and the best ways of composting. The visitors include Israelis who want the farm to prosper. As the Israeli newspaper Haaretz reported, "They [visiting Israelis] lined the farm's trails with car tires, which Al-Kufash calls 'dew traps' since the rubber's temperature shifts between day and night, producing dew."[4]

Kids visit to learn about farming and growing their own food. The farm also brings people together for a sense of community and to teach younger people about their farming heritage.[5]

A Palestinian bride and groom on their wedding day. The bride is pinned with paper money which is traditionally given as wedding gifts to the couple.

CHAPTER 7
Let's Celebrate!

Even though life in Palestine can be difficult and often dangerous, Palestinians are like people everywhere. They value religion, family, home, and heritage, and one of the best ways to show this is through their own special set of holidays, festivals, and celebrations. Because family plays such a big role in their lives, marking family milestones is especially important.

When a baby is born, family and friends will visit for weeks to offer their congratulations and best wishes to the parents and grandparents. Families celebrate births with a ceremony called an *aqeeqah*. Animals are slaughtered, and the meat is shared with family, friends, and people in need. They also serve a traditional dessert called *mughli*, a pudding made of semolina flour, sugar, and cinnamon, topped with fresh nuts. Because Palestinian society is based on men as the head of the household, the birth of a son is generally celebrated more than the birth of a daughter. Sons are usually named after their grandfather on their father's side of the family.

When Palestinians marry, boys are usually in their early 20s but girls might be as young as 16 or 18. In villages and rural areas, the fathers of the bride and groom might arrange the marriage. The daughter is often allowed to meet the potential groom and decide whether to accept him. In cities, couples may do more dating, but often with a chaperone from their family.

Weddings are huge celebrations, often lasting three days, with hundreds of guests. Fathers, brothers, male cousins, and uncles give the bride gold necklaces or bracelets. The groom gives his bride gifts of gold, called *shabkeh*, as a sign of his family's wealth. The new couple also receives money from the wedding guests to help them start their new lives together.

Palestine has both national and religious holidays. One national holiday is Labor Day on May 1. Another is Independence Day on November 15, which marks the date in 1988 when PLO chairman Yasser Arafat proclaimed that Palestine was free. On Independence Day, Palestinians organize demonstrations, wave Palestinian flags, and make speeches about the history of Palestine and their hope for recognition as an independent country. These days are usually celebrated with a day off from school and work.

Muslim religious holidays include Eid al-Adha, the Feast of the Sacrifice. It takes place at the end of the annual Hajj, or pilgrimage to Mecca, the Islamic holy center. Muslim families may slaughter a sheep and share it with family, friends, and less fortunate people. Children receive gifts like new clothes and money.

Palestinian Christians celebrate Christmas with gifts, carol singing, and traditional foods like roast lamb, candy made with nougat and sesame seeds, roasted chestnuts, a hot sweet drink of rosewater and nuts, and semolina pancakes stuffed with nuts and cheese. Many join a special procession in Bethlehem on Christmas Eve. It ends in Manger Square, where Jesus is believed to have been born. Easter is celebrated with processions into and around Jerusalem, marking the final days of the life of Jesus.

There are other celebrations in Palestine that aren't specifically holidays. The olive harvest in the autumn is a time to be thankful for the crop of olives, used as food and to make olive oil. Olive trees are also an important symbol of Palestine. They are an ancient symbol of peace, and represent connection

Young Palestinian Christian boys watch the traditional Christmas Eve procession in Manger Square in Bethlehem. Thousands of people visit this West Bank town every Christmas.

to the land and to generations before that may have planted them. A 13-year old Palestinian named Shahed said, "For us, the olive harvest is even better than a wedding. It's when the land comes alive again, and the trees bear jewels."[1]

Celebrations don't necessarily mean just specific events and activities. Palestine also has its own stories, songs, and superstitions that maintain its culture and pass it along. Palestinian artisans create beautiful pottery, leather and wooden goods, and paintings. Islam discourages art that depicts people or animals, so most designs feature geometric patterns, plants, and leaves. Artists skilled at calligraphy, an elaborate type of writing, often illustrate verses from the Qur'an, the Islamic holy book. Women embroider clothing, pillows, and tablecloths in an ancient form of cross-stitch.

Songs and dancing are an important part of the culture as well. There are songs for every important occasion, led by singers called *zajjaleen*. The traditional dance, called the *dabka*, is performed with handkerchiefs and stomping feet.

Palestinian youths perform the *dabka*, a Palestinian folk dance, as they participate in the Olive Harvest Festival in the West Bank city of Bethlehem.

Palestine has fostered many writers and poets. Older works include stories of the Prophet Muhammad's journeys and teachings, as well as traditional Arabic stories like *1001 Nights*. Notable modern Palestinian writers include poets Mahmoud Darwish and Fouzi al-Asmar, and novelist Emile Habibi. Some writers have been forced to move away from Palestine. They include Edward Said, Liana Badr, and Hassan al-Kanafani.

Palestine may be a difficult place to live, with the constant conflict between Palestine and Israel, and the violence and political problems that go with it. But the Palestinian people are strongly connected to their land, their religion, their families, and their heritage. As long as they have those values, Palestine will continue to be their home.

RAMADAN

While it really isn't a celebration, Ramadan is one of the most important Islamic observances. It lasts for the entire length of the month of Ramadan, which is either 29 or 30 days long. During that time, most Muslims fast during daylight hours. That means they cannot eat or drink during this time. They believe that fasting cleanses the body and the soul.

Some groups are excused from fasting. They include those who are seriously ill, the aged, young children, and nursing or pregnant women. In recent years, professional athletes have been allowed to skip fasting on the days when they have major competitions, though they have to make them up later.

Because Islam uses the lunar calendar, which is 354 days long, the time in which the month of Ramadan falls continually changes from year to year. The fasting can be especially difficult when Ramadan occurs in mid-summer, with daylight in some areas lasting for 16, 17, or 18 hours or even longer. In winter the period of dawn to dusk is much shorter.

Family gatherings are very important, and people often invite friends to share the evening meal that takes place after the sun sets. Men usually visit the mosque every evening for special prayers. Women receive gifts of money (*eidayyas*) from their male relatives during Ramadan. Ramadan ends with Eid al-Fitr, the Fast-Breaking Feast.

A Palestinian boy reads verses from the Qur'an during Ramadan.

HARISSA

Harissa is a semolina dessert. It can be served warm or cold. This recipe involves using the stove and oven. Be sure to always have **an adult** help you in the kitchen!

Ingredients

3 cups semolina flour (Cream of Wheat cereal can be substituted, but the cake will have a grittier consistency)
1¼ cup sugar
½ cup butter (one stick), softened
2 cups plain yogurt
1 cup shredded coconut
1 teaspoon baking soda
Tahini, a paste of ground sesame seeds that looks like peanut butter*
Sugar syrup
2 cups water
3 cups sugar

Instructions

1. Preheat oven to 350 degrees.
2. In a large bowl, mix the semolina, sugar, butter, and yogurt until smooth.
3. Add coconut and mix well.
4. Add baking soda and mix.
5. Cover the bottom and sides of a 9½ by 13 inch pan with a thin layer of tahini.
6. Spread the semolina mixture in the pan.
7. Bake for 30 minutes, or until cake is brownish in color.
8. Remove cake from oven and cool slightly.
9. Meanwhile, mix the water and sugar in a saucepan. With an adult's help, heat to boiling stirring constantly, until it thickens into a syrup. Watch very carefully so it does not burn or boil over!
10. Cut the harissa into small pieces, and pour the syrup over it.

*Available in the specialty section of grocery stores or organic food stores

EMBROIDERED BOOKMARK

Palestinian women are noted for their beautiful embroidery. You can create a bookmark using two traditional Palestinian patterns. Remember, have **an adult** help you!

Materials

Aida cloth, 6 or 8 count size
Embroidery floss, 2 colors
Embroidery hoop
Embroidery needle, #22 or #24
   (should have a blunt tip)
Felt square in a matching color
Scissors
White glue

Instructions

1. Cut a piece of Aida cloth approximately 10 by 10 inches. You can put masking tape around the edges to keep it from fraying.
2. Fold the cloth gently in half to make a crease. This is the center of the pattern.
3. Cut a length of floss about 12 inches long. Separate three strands of floss from the length. You will stitch with three strands at a time.
4. Look at the pattern. Start with the long "stem" of the tree. Stitch an x in the squares marked in the pattern, by coming up at the lower left corner of the square, down in the upper right corner, up in the upper left corner, and down in the lower right corner. As you stitch, catch the end of the thread on the back side of the cloth with your stitches, to anchor the thread so it won't come out.
5. Follow the pattern using one color for the tree and another for the center of the leaves. Use these same two colors for the border.
6. When you are done stitching, trim the Aida cloth a half inch from your stitching. Cut a rectangle of felt that is slightly wider and several inches longer than your Aida cloth and stitching.
7. Glue the Aida stitching to the felt strip and let dry. You've made a beautiful Palestinian bookmark using the False Tree and the Stick border patterns!

WHAT YOU SHOULD KNOW ABOUT PALESTINE

Area: 2,402 square miles (6,220 square kilometers)
Climate: hot summers, cooler and more moderate winters
National symbol: olive tree
Average age: 17
Population: 4,440,127
Language: Arabic
Religion: Muslim, some Christians
Did you know?

- Palestinians who have fled to another country form one of the largest refugee groups in the world.
- Children are very important in Palestinian culture, and Palestine has one of the highest birth rates in the world.
- Gaza City, founded in 3000 BCE, is one of the oldest cities in the world
- Muslim sons are responsible for taking care of their mothers and sisters unless they have money to care for themselves.
- Palestinians must carry Israeli-issued ID cards and cannot leave the Palestinian Territories without permission
- Palestinians only call their close friends by their first names. Everyone else is addressed by title (such as Miss, Mrs. or Mr.) and their last name.

Flag: The Palestinian flag is based on the flag of the 1916 Arab Revolt against Ottoman rule. The horizontal stripes represent three early Islamic dynasties. The red triangle represents the Hashemite dynasty, which was descended from Muhammad and controlled Muslim holy sites for many centuries.

TIMELINE

Dates BCE

9000s	Jericho, the earliest known settlement in the region, is established.
3000s	Settlements on the site of Gaza City are established.
1000	Hebrews establish the kingdom of Israel.
587	Babylonians destroy the temple in Jerusalem and take most of the Hebrews into captivity.
538	Hebrews return to Jerusalem and begin rebuilding the temple.
332	Greek general Alexander the Great conquers the region.
63	Roman forces seize Jerusalem and kill thousands of Jews.

Dates CE

70	The Romans destroy the rebuilt temple in Jerusalem.
100s	The Romans expel the Jews and rename the area as Syria Palestina.
636	Muslim Arabs conquer the region of Palestine.
1096	Christian crusaders from Europe capture the Holy Land from the Arabs.
1187	Saladin leads the Muslim recapture of the Holy Land.
1517	Palestine becomes part of the Ottoman Empire
1832	Egypt takes control of Palestine, but it reverts to Ottoman control eight years later.
1882	The first wave of Jewish settlers from Europe arrives in Palestine.
1897	Zionism declares its goal of establishing a Jewish state in Palestine.
1914	World War I begins.
1917	With the Balfour Declaration, Britain declares its intention to create a Jewish homeland in Palestine.
1922	The League of Nations approves the British Mandate for Palestine.
1936–1939	The Arab Revolt protests against British Mandate and Jewish settlements.
1939	World War II begins and lasts until 1945.
1947	The United Nations votes to divide Palestine into two nations, one for the Jews and one for the Arabs.
1948	Britain withdraws from Palestine; Israel declares itself a state.
1949	The loss of the Arab-Israeli War leaves about 750,000 Palestinians with no homeland.
1964	The Palestine Liberation Organization (PLO) is established.
1967	Israel takes over the West Bank, Gaza Strip and all of Jerusalem with its victory in the Six-Day War.
1969	Yasser Arafat becomes chairman of the PLO.
1988	The First Intifada begins.
1993	Israel and the PLO sign the Oslo Peace Accords.
1994	Israel allows Palestinians to govern themselves in the Gaza Strip and Jericho
2000	The Second Intifada begins.
2002	Israel begins construction of a security wall around the West Bank.
2005	Israeli and Palestinian leaders announce a cease-fire to end the Second Intifada.
2012	The United Nations admits Palestine as a non-member observer.
2013	The two leading political parties (Hamas and Fatah) sign an agreement to try to work together.
2014	The United Nations declares 2014 as The Year of Solidarity with the Palestinian People

CHAPTER NOTES

Chapter 1: A Day in the Life

1. Bahaa Interview, *CultureGrams Online Edition.* ProQuest, January 26, 2014.

2. Bahaa Interview.

3. Author interview with Murad Al Kufash, Marda Village, Palestine. December 2, 2013.

4. Bahaa Interview.

5. "One Palestinian child has been killed by Israel every 3 days for the past 13 years." Middle East Monitor, June 4, 2013. https://www.middleeastmonitor.com/news/middle-east/6185-one-palestinian-child-has-been-killed-by-israel-every-3-days-for-the-past-13-years

6. "UN official: Israeli occupation killed 1,300 Palestinian children since 2000." Middle East Monitor, May 4, 2011. https://www.middleeastmonitor.com/news/middle-east/2300-un-official-israeli-occupation-killed-1300-palestinian-children-since-2000

7. Author interview with Nicholas Robson, December 2, 2013.

8. "UNICEF Concerned About Impact of Violence on Palestinian and Israeli Children." UNICEF, November 15, 2001. http://www.unicef.org/newsline/01pr87.htm

Chapter 2: Looking Around

1. Rania Filfil and Barbara Louton, "The Other Face of Gaza: The Gaza Continuum," This Week in Palestine, September, 2008. http://www.thisweekinpalestine.com/details.php?id=2564&ed=157&edid=157

2. Geography of Palestine, State of Palestine: Permanent Observer Mission to the United Nations. http://www.un.int/wcm/content/site/palestine/cache/offonce/pid/11598;jsessionid=75E12AE0367B43DECE3357D9120E27CF

3. Gaza, CIA World Factbook, https://www.cia.gov/library/publications/the-world-factbook/geos/gz.html; West Bank, CIA World Factbook, https://www.cia.gov/library/publications/the-world-factbook/geos/we.html

4. Alia Hoyt, "Is the Dead Sea really dead?" HowStuffWorks.com. http://geography.howstuffworks.com/oceans-and-seas/dead-sea-dead.htm

Chapter 3: A Land at the Crossroads

1. Amy Dockser Marcus, *Jerusalem 1913: The Origins of the Arab-Israeli Conflict* (New York: Viking, 2007), p. 77.

2. "The Balfour Declaration of 1917," History Learning Site. http://www.historylearningsite.co.uk/balfour_declaration_2.htm

3. Mike Konrad, "The White Paper of 1939." *American Thinker*, June 2, 2013. http://www.americanthinker.com/2013/06/the_white_paper_of_1939.html

4. Esmail Nashif, *Palestinian Political Prisoners: Identity and Community* (Oxford, United Kingdom: Routledge, 2008), p. 24.

CHAPTER NOTES

5. David Margolick, "Endless War: A Review of 1948: A History of the First Arab-Israeli War." *New York Times*, May 4, 2008. http://www.nytimes.com/2008/05/04/books/review/Margolick-t.html?pagewanted=all&_r=0

6. Ibid.

Chapter 4: Conflict and Occupation

1. Brian Handwerk, "What Does 'Jihad' Really Mean to Muslims?" *National Geographic*, October 23, 2003. http://news.nationalgeographic.com/news/2003/10/1023_031023_jihad.html

Chapter Five: Living in Palestine

1. "High unemployment blights Palestinian lives—UN Report." UN News Center, August 24, 2011. http://www.un.org/apps/news/story.asp/html/story.asp?NewsID=39373&Cr=palestin&Cr1=

2. "Report: Hamas and the Palestinian Authority in talks to form unity government," *Jerusalem Post*, December 17, 2013. http://www.jpost.com/Middle-East/Report-Hamas-and-the-Palestinian-Authority-in-talks-to-form-unity-government-335262

3. Legal Consequences of the Construction of a Wall in the Occupied Palestinian Territory. The International Court of Justice, July 9, 2004. http://www.icj-cij.org/docket/index.php?pr=71&p1=3&p2=1&case=131&p3=6

Chapter Six: At Home

1. Hanadi. Interview. *CultureGrams Online Edition*. ProQuest, 2014. January 26, 2014.

2. Murad Al-Kufash, from Marda Village, Palestine. Interview, December 2, 2013.

3. Karen Chernick, "Marda Permaculture Farm Plans Sustainable Seeds in Palestine." Green Prophet: Sustainable News for the Middle East, October 22, 2010. http://www.greenprophet.com/2010/10/marda-permaculture-farm-palestine/#sthash.P20O3BDR.dpuf

4. Yuval Ben-Ami, "Sustainability in the shadow of a West Bank settlement." *Haaretz*, September 23, 2012. http://www.haaretz.com/news/features/sustainability-in-the-shadow-of-a-west-bank-settlement-1.466384

5. Marda Permaculture Farm. http://mardafarm.com/

Chapter Seven: Let's Celebrate!

1. Catherine Weibel, "Ancient autumn ritual brings joy and pride to Palestinian children." At a glance: State of Palestine, UNICEF. http://www.unicef.org/infobycountry/oPt_60644.html

FURTHER READING

Books

Carew-Miller, Anna. *The Palestinians*. Broomall, PA: Mason Crest Publishers, 2004.

Gonzales, Todd. *Palestine in the News: Past, Present, and Future*. Berkeley Heights, NJ: Enslow Publishers, 2006.

Mason, Paul. *Global Hotspots: Israel and Palestine*. New York: Cavendish Square Publishing, 2008.

Sharp, Anne Wallace. *The Palestinians*. Farmington Hills, MI: Lucent Books, 2005.

Wingate, Katherine. *The Intifadas*. New York: Rosen Publishing, 2003.

Works Consulted
Books and Periodicals

Ben-Ami, Yuval. "Sustainability in the shadow of a West Bank settlement." *Haaretz*, September 23, 2012. http://www.haaretz.com/news/features/sustainability-in-the-shadow-of-a-west-bank-settlement-1.466384

Carter, Jimmy. *Palestine: Peace Not Apartheid*. New York: Simon & Schuster, 2006.

Chernick, Karen. "Marda Permaculture Farm Plans Sustainable Seeds in Palestine." Green Prophet: Sustainable News for the Middle East, October 22, 2010. http://www.greenprophet.com/2010/10/marda-permaculture-farm-palestine/#sthash.P20O3BDR.dpuf

Filfil, Rania and Barbara Louton, "The Other Face of Gaza: The Gaza Continuum," This Week in Palestine, September, 2008. http://www.thisweekinpalestine.com/details.php?id=2564&ed=157&edid=157

Frank, Mitchell. *Understanding the Holy Land: Answering Questions About the Israeli-Palestinian Conflict*. New York: Penguin Books, 2005.

Handwerk, Brian. "What Does 'Jihad' Really Mean to Muslims?" *National Geographic*, October 23, 2003. http://news.nationalgeographic.com/news/2003/10/1023_031023_jihad.html

Konrad, Mike. "The White Paper of 1939." *American Thinker*, June 2, 2013. http://www.americanthinker.com/2013/06/the_white_paper_of_1939.html

Lewis, Bernard. *Notes on a Century: Reflections of a Middle East Historian*. New York: Penguin Books, 2012.

Mansfield, Peter. *A History of the Middle East*, 4th Edition. New York: Penguin Books, 2013.

Marcus, Amy Docker. *Jerusalem 1913: The Origins of the Arab-Israeli Conflict*. New York: Viking, 2007.

Margolick, David. "Endless War: A Review of 1948: A History of the First Arab-Israeli War." *New York Times*, May 4, 2008. http://www.nytimes.com/2008/05/04/books/review/Margolick-t.html?pagewanted=all&_r=0

Nashif, Esmail. *Palestinian Political Prisoners: Identity and Community*. Oxford, United Kingdom: Routledge, 2008.

Sacco, Joe. *Palestine*. Seattle, WA: Fantagraphic Books, 2001.

Interviews

Author interview with Murad al Kufash, December 2, 2013, Los Cocos, Cuba.

Author interview with Nicholas Robson, December 2, 2013, Los Cocos, Cuba.

FURTHER READING

On the Internet

The Balfour Declaration of 1917. History Learning Site http://www.historylearningsite. co.uk/balfour_declaration_2.htm

Countries and Their Culture: Palestine, West Bank, and Gaza Strip http://www.everyculture.com/No-Sa/Palestine-West-Bank-and-Gaza-Strip.html

CultureGrams World Edition 2014: West Bank and Gaza. www.proquestk12.com (subscription)

Fact Monster: Palestinian State http://www.factmonster.com/ipka/A0776421.html

Gaza. The CIA World Factbook. https://www.cia.gov/library/publications/the-world-factbook/geos/gz.html

"Geography of Palestine." State of Palestine, Permanent Observer Mission to the United Nations. http://www.un.int/wcm/content/site/palestine/cache/offonce/pid/11598;jsessionid=75E12AE0367B43DECE3357D9120E27CF

"High unemployment blights Palestinian lives—UN Report." UN News Center, August 24, 2011. http://www.un.org/apps/news/story.asp/html/story.asp?NewsID=39373&Cr=palestin&Cr1=

Hoyt, Alia. "Is the Dead Sea really dead?" HowStuffWorks.com. http://geography.howstuffworks.com/oceans-and-seas/dead-sea-dead.htm

Legal Consequences of the Construction of a Wall in the Occupied Palestinian Territory. The International Court of Justice, July 9, 2004. http://www.icj-cij.org/docket/index.php?pr=71&p1=3&p2=1&case=131&p3=6

Maps of the World: Palestine http://www.mapsofworld.com/palestine/society-and-culture/

Marda Permaculture Farm www.mardafarm.com

Moore, John. "The evolution of Islamic Terrorism: an overview." PBS Frontline. http://www.pbs.org/wgbh/pages/frontline/shows/target/etc/modern.html

Palestine, West Bank, and Gaza Strip. Countries and Their Cultures. http://www.everyculture.com/No-Sa/Palestine-West-Bank-and-Gaza-Strip.html

"Report: Hamas and the Palestinian Authority in talks to form unity government," *Jerusalem Post*, December 17, 2013. http://www.jpost.com/Middle-East/Report-Hamas-and-the-Palestinian-Authority-in-talks-to-form-unity-government-335262

Weibel, Catherine. "Ancient autumn ritual brings joy and pride to Palestinian children." At a glance: State of Palestine, UNICEF. http://www.unicef.org/infobycountry/oPt_60644.html

West Bank. The CIA World Factbook. https://www.cia.gov/library/publications/the-world-factbook/geos/we.html

"Wildlife of Palestine.: Wide World: Natural history from around the world. http://iberianature.com/wildworld/guides/wildlife-in-palestine/

GLOSSARY

annex (AN-eks)—Add territory to an existing country.

archaeological (ahr-kee-uh-LAH-jih-kuhl)—Having to do with studying artifacts and ruins of previous civilizations.

boycott (BOI-kaht)—To stop having commercial or social relations with another country or group as a way of punishing them or protesting certain actions.

checkpoint (CHEK-point)—A barrier or gate at a border where travelers go through security checks.

conflict (KAHN-flikt)—A war, seriousness disagreement, or argument.

corrugated (KOHR-uh-gated)—A material or surface shaped into wavy ridges and grooves

descendant (dee-SEHN-duhnt)—A person, plant, or animal that comes from a specific ancestor.

dialect (DY-uh-lekt)—A version of a language spoken by a group living in a particular region.

dispute (di-SPYOOT)—A disagreement, argument, or debate.

geographical (jee-uh-GRAF-ih-kuhl)—Having to do with the natural features of a region.

immigrate (IHM-uh-grate)—To come to a foreign country and live there permanently.

jihad (jee-HAWD)—Acts of violence used to avenge acts that have supposedly hurt Muslims.

mandate (MAN-date)—An official order to do something.

migration (my-GRAY-shun)—The seasonal movements of animals and birds from one region to another.

mosque (MAHSK)—A Muslim place of worship.

occupation (aw-kyu-PAY-shun)—When one country occupies or controls another country.

pita bread (PEE-tuh BREHD)—Thin, flat bread baked in a round shape.

sewage (SOO-ij)—Waste water and human waste.

sponsor (SPAWN-suhr)—To provide support for a project or activity.

tolerate (TAHL-uhr-ate)—To allow something to be done without interfering.

INDEX

About the Author

Marcia Amidon Lusted has written 90 books and over 450 articles for young readers. She is also a children's magazine editor and a musician. In 2013, she met and made friends with a Palestinian and learned a great deal about his family, culture, and what it's really like to live in the West Bank.

PALESTINE